Art Journaling for Beginners

100+ Prompts to Teach You What and How to Journal

by Rachel Ramey

Introduction to the Print Edition

The print edition of this book (like the PDF edition) contains the same prompts as the Kindle edition. However, the formatting is different. This edition is designed so the book may be read book-style as-is *or* the prompts may be copied onto cardstock and cut to make a deck of prompt *cards*. If you do this, you may want to copy each category onto a different *color* of cardstock, so you can tell them apart at a glance on occasions when it's relevant to you.

The PDF edition contains the same formatting as this print edition. (The PDF edition does contain hyperlinks which, for obvious reasons, are not present here.)

What is an Art Journal?

An art journal is a thing that's hard to define because, by nature, every artist's art journal will be different. But at its most basic, an art journal is a journal that incorporates both words (journaling/writing) and images.

Art journals often incorporate doodles, sketching, collages, paint and other media, and tend to make use of multiple layers on any given page.

There is no "right way" to work in an art journal, but some of us are new enough to this non-linear and/or artistic way of thinking, that we need someone to tell us what to do or we can't even get started!

That is the purpose of these prompts: use them to get you started. If you're completely new to art journaling, I hope the ideas will teach you some skills you can expand on as you grow your journal. If you're an experienced art journaler, perhaps they will be useful when you have "writer's block."

Because they are aimed at beginners, the majority of these prompts are designed to *not* require any fancy art supplies. They *do* require supplies, but they call for supplies of the inexpensive variety that most elementary-school teachers would have around: markers, magazines to tear up, colored pencils, watercolors, etc.

Of course, you will also require a blank journal or some other paper to journal on, and a few of the projects call for slightly more specialized supplies, such as acrylic paints (craft acrylics are fine) or correction fluid. I've avoided any projects that require expensive supplies such as gouache or gesso, because I assume that most readers will not want to invest in these until they've given art journaling a solid try and decided it's something they wish to continue with.

So grab a journal, pick a prompt – any prompt; they don't have to be used in order – and jump in!

The Prompts:

(beginning on the following page)

Baby Steps

1. Segment a page. Write in the segments. (Hint: You don't have to make the segments the same size or shape, and you don't necessarily have to write the same size, direction, or in the same "font" in each one.) BONUS: Can you create other pages that use the same prompt, but create the segments in other ways? [horizontal stripes, horizontal wavy stripes, boxes, vertical stripes, rows of circles, a combination…]	2. Glue down a page of text. Write and/or draw on top of it.
3. Use a variety of *lines* – horizontal, vertical, diagonal; straight, curvy, zig-zaggy; thick, thin.	4. Pick a (simple) shape – dots, hearts, diamonds, etc. – and use color to fill in the spaces around your writing with just this one shape.

5. Pick a single color and use it to embellish your page.	6. Journal first. (Don't write too tiny.) Go back and decorate some of the individual words or phrases.
7. Draw something around you – anything you can see in your immediate space. Now fill in around the picture with words.	8. Use stencils. How many ways can you think of to use a stencil for your art journal? For creating a background? For painting inside to make a design element? For writing inside? For making an *inside-out* design element (painting/drawing/ coloring everywhere *but* inside the stencil)? For drawing over top of existing journaling or page prep? …

9. Use rubber stamps.	10. Ink the edges of the page. BONUS: Ink the edges of a page you have already painted or otherwise prepped.
11. Trace over what you have written or doodled in black, with colors. (Colored pencils over Sharpie, for instance.)	12. Take a shortcut to Zentangle®-inspired art – use a rubber stamp to stamp a black-and-white image. Now fill in the spaces with repetitive doodled patterns in black ink. (If your stamp is relatively small, you may need to stamp it multiple times on the page and/or use multiple stamps.)

13. Stick sticky notes onto the page. You can use neat rows or not – whatever you like. Now paint over the page. Let it dry, then remove the notes.

14. Stick a magazine cutout onto the page (or hold it firmly in place). Paint over the page, then remove the cutout. (Tip: You can save your cutouts and reuse them.)

15. What else can you use for "masking" a page prior to painting, besides sticky notes and magazine cutouts?

16. Use an old (used-up!) gift card to scrape acrylic paint all over a page.

17. Sponge-paint a page.

18. Splatter-paint a page.

19. Spread a page with watercolors. Sprinkle with salt while it's wet.

20. Apply drops of watercolor to a page that is already thoroughly wet with plain water. They should run together.

BONUS: Wet the whole page with a wash of *color*, then drop on paint in an analogous hue.

21. Using a very fluid paint or ink, add some "pools" to the edge of a page. (Start with a little the first time, until you see how much you need, so you don't pour it all over your workspace!) Now hold the page on end, with the "pools" at the top of the page so they run down.

22. Using two facing pages you want to prep, add one or more "blobs" of paint to one side. Close the book and press the pages together, then open them up and let them dry.

23. Paint a page in multiple layers. Use a first layer (or more) that provides an overall background. Then stamp over it, spread it with paint using a different technique, paint a picture on it, or use one of the masking techniques.

24. Create an ombre design. Paint a rough stripe of a color at the top, bottom, or to one side of your page. Add a little white or black to your paint, and paint the next stripe down (or up, or over – whichever direction you're going). Add a little more of the white/black and paint the next stripe. Continue until your page is filled.

25. Tear strips of patterned or printed paper (magazine pages work well) and glue them onto the page in stripes to cover the background. You can trim the edges even, or leave them to stick off the page. Make them all shades of the same color, use a particular color scheme, or let them be "all over the map."

BONUS: Glue pieces on in another pattern, like a grid or weave or checkerboard.

26. Find some paper with an interesting print, like a map or graph paper, and glue it down as a background. If you like, paint over it with watercolors or a thin wash of acrylics to add some color.

27. Use a pencil eraser to stamp dots on a page somewhere. You can use them to make a border, use them as a background, use them to decorate between words, use them *as* the words…whatever you choose.

28. Drizzle rubber cement on a page, and let it dry. Paint the page with the method of your choosing. Peel off the rubber cement.

29. Use crayons to draw on a page, before using watercolors to paint the whole thing. If you want the crayons to be part of the design, use colored ones. If you just want blank space to show, use white ones (or whatever color your paper is), or clear wax crayons from an egg-decorating kit. (Of course, if you can't readily *write* over the crayon, either, so you'll need to use something like gesso over areas you want to write on, once it's dry. If you don't have gesso, try white-out.)

30. Use "found objects" to stamp with. (That is, stamp with something other than stamps.)

31. Find at least three different papers. Tear pieces from them and glue them down as the "base" of your page. (If you like, you can then paint over them using one of the paint-based background-prep. techniques.)

32. "Tie-dye" your page: use colored Sharpies to make dots on the page in shapes roughly corresponding to the shapes you want to end up with. (Like a pointillism.) Then spritz with rubbing alcohol to make the ink bleed. Allow to dry. (Be sure to protect the underlying pages when you spray!) Note: Depending on the properties of your regular journaling paper, this may or may not work directly on the page. You may need to use a very porous paper like paper toweling or coffee filters for the "tie-dye" effect and glue it in after it dries. Experiment!

33. Use lots of tiny scraps to "tile" a page.

34. How many different ways can you doodle a: heart, star, flower, circle, swirl, leaf…

35. Make a pattern page. Divide the page into small squares and draw a different pattern inside each one.

BONUS: Can you do a whole page of patterns using only straight lines and a whole page of patterns using only curvy lines?

36. Create a page of border ideas.

BONUS: You could save border ideas you find elsewhere by gluing them into your book.

BONUS 2: Can you use a glued-in border as the start of a page design?

37. Create a page of different lettering styles.

BONUS: You could save lettering ideas you find elsewhere by gluing them into your book.

38. Draw stitching on a page. How many kinds of stitching can you think of to draw? How many ways can you use faux stitching? To outline a page? To outline an element? To create text? To define sections of a page? To add embellishment to a page element? (You don't have to use these all on a single page!)

39. Find a patterned fabric. Copy the pattern onto a segment of your page. (Or use it as inspiration and draw a *similar* pattern.)

40. Add fingerprints to a page. Use pens to add details, turning them into little pictures.

41. Use a page with horizontal lines on it – either inherent to the paper, or drawn on; straight or curvy. Now write your journaling between the lines in such a way that the letters reach all the way to the lines above and below them. (Fill the space!)

Doodling/Lettering Practice

42. Create a doodle page: Draw a basic shape to outline your space (perhaps a rectangle or circle). Divide it into multiple spaces of varying shapes. Fill each section with a (different) repetitive pattern. (Then you can add color as you like.)

43. Choose a subject – a fairly simple subject, but more complex than a basic shape. A tree, maybe, or a bird…Draw it as many *different* ways as you can think of.

44. Choose a page you've already worked on. Embellish it with one or more mostly-flat-but-3-dimensional objects, like buttons, brads, foam stickers, etc.	45. Add ribbon, yarn, twine, or similar fiber to a page.
46. Add tabs to a page.	47. Begin with a page you have prepared with a painted background. Glue on a magazine image (or similar cutout). Draw/doodle on the magazine image with a bold marker.

48. Cut out a fairly large magazine picture. Chop it so that it is an incomplete image, then glue it into your book. Draw on the page to complete the image. Hint: The newly-completed image does *not* have to match the original, or even be realistic/make sense. In fact, it may be more fun if it doesn't!	49. Draw a speech bubble or thought bubble on plain paper. Cut it out, leaving the outline intact. Add this to a journal page.
50. Using decorative punches, punch out designs from separate paper (solid, patterned, textured, or magazine-type pages). Add these to your book. –OR– punch holes *out* of your pages and use the blank space as part of your design. (Or both!)	51. Create a cut-out and add something behind it.

52. Create your own rubber stamp. If you're ambitious, you can carve it from an eraser with real stamp-carving tools or an X-Acto knife. (Be careful!) If you're less ambitious – or just want something larger – try cutting it from craft foam (in which case you'll probably need to adhere it to something firm).

53. Use three or more of the techniques from other prompts, in the same page.

54. Add pressed leaves or flowers to a page.

55. Add something metallic.

56. Use glitter.	57. Use fabric in a page.
58. Sew on a page. (You can sew something *to* the page, or you can just sew on the page itself.)	59. Glue in something random you've collected that you love – a candy wrapper with a great quote, the fortune from a fortune cookie, a great illustration from a shopping bag, etc. Let this play a key role in the finished page.

60. Use a large shaped punch to create a number of "punchies" of the same size and shape (but not necessarily color/pattern/texture). Arrange these in a "grid"-type pattern on your page and use as the basis of the page. If you are happy with them as the centerpiece, then feel free to just embellish. Or use them as segments of the page for journaling/doodling in/on.

61. Create a face and/or an outfit that is a composite of cut-out magazine images. For instance, cut out eyes from a couple of magazine photos, nose from one, mouth from another, etc. and create your face. Or collage an outfit from one image's top, another's skirt, another's shoes, etc. Embellish the finished image with drawn-on details and/or with other materials.

62. Glue in a photograph. (If you're a kid, be sure it's one you're allowed to use!) Draw/write on it or over it.

63. Add rubbings to a page.

64. Add tissue paper. Note that colored tissue paper will bleed when moistened (even with liquid glue). You can use this to your advantage with page preparation if you like. White tissue paper can be glued as a "film" over too-dark backgrounds, to provide a more subtle backdrop for journaling. Experiment with gluing in page-size sheets and smaller pieces, and with gluing them in smoothly or scrunching/wrinkling them first.

65. Plain white (or brown) paper toweling can add interesting texture to a page. Try gluing it in before prepping a page with paints, inks, etc. (It also lets markers bleed, so you could experiment with using markers for page prep over a paper towel.)

66. Use foil in a layout.

67. Punch holes with something small like a needle or an awl.

68. Using water-soluble markers, scribble on a section of scrap paper. Using a dampened stamp, dip into the marker scribble to ink your stamp, then use it to stamp on your page. The result should be a watercolor-like effect.

69. "Inchies" are one-inch-by-one-inch pieces of art, of whatever variety. Create a page of inchies – either drawn/doodled or cut out from magazines, etc.	70. Collect miscellaneous clippings and/or ephemera. Grab a random piece, and challenge yourself to make a page around a quote or Scripture using it.
71. Cut out a magazine photo and glue it onto your page. Write over it and/or around it. You can even write on it, in the *space* around it, *and* outline it with text.	72. Try creating your page in negative. Imagine decorating a stencil, then laying that stencil on top of a blank sheet of paper. The primary content should be communicated through the "white space," with your writing/artwork filling in everything else, as though it were the tangible portion of the stencil. (One way to do this would be to create your content as a "mask," paint or otherwise decorate over it, then remove the mask. You might come up with a more creative way to tackle this challenge, though!)

73. Fill a whole page with large circles, boxes, hearts, or some other simple shape. Fill some with doodles/designs and others with your text/lettering.

74. Choose a page that has large lettering (a single quote or something, rather than a full page of small journaling). If you feel you need them to separate the text from the background, add lines to accomplish this. Then decorate the background between the text.

75. Glue a dictionary page in as a page background. Choose one or more words/definitions from the page to highlight, and make them the focal point of your page design. You could white/black everything else out, you could outline these, you could doodle on the topic, etc…or some combination of techniques.

76. Create one doodled image in the middle of a large, otherwise-blank white page. Just leave the rest of the space blank.

77. Trace around your hand, foot, or other simple, recognizable object (such as a pair of scissors) one or more times.

BONUS: Write your journaling around the edges of these outlines.

78. Trace around several *un*recognizable objects to add interest to a page. (This could be part of your background preparation, as well.)

79. Glue in a newspaper page. Create your own poetry or other journaling by covering up or blacking out the words you *don't* want and keeping those you do.

80. Collage a page so it's completely full. Then choose an image to use as a mask and paint over the whole collage with a solid color before removing the mask.

Subject Matter

81. Favorite quote or Scripture verse.	82. A single letter of the alphabet.
83. A particular color. (Choose one randomly.)	84. Freewriting – don't think. Just set the timer for a set amount of time and write whatever comes into your head (even if it doesn't make sense and/or isn't complete sentences!) Or instead of setting a timer you could decide you're going to fill up one page or some other set number of pages or sections of a page.

85. Free*drawing*. You know what freewriting is, right? (If not, see card #84.) Try drawing the same way.

86. Two sides of something: positives and negatives; things you hate, things you love; things you worry about, what God says about them…you get the idea.

87. Your to-do list.

88. Your grocery list.

89.   Things that make you happy.

90.   Lists: anything you can think to make a list of.

BONUS: How many different formats can you use to present a list?

91.   Make a page of ways you like to relax/take a break/enjoy yourself.

92.   The contents of your purse (or wallet, or backpack, or…)

Subject Matter

93. Use a photocopy machine (or scanner) to blow up your thumbprint to page-sized. Glue it to the page and use it as the focal point.

94. Create a page about your favorite variety of some very ordinary/everyday object, such as your favorite shampoo.

95. Create a page about your favorite things – but don't use words to create it (except, perhaps, as embellishments). Use objects, drawings, magazine images, etc.

96. Choose 3-5 random words from the dictionary. Use them together in a page.

97. Choose 3-5 random images clipped from magazines. Use them together in a page.	98. Today's weather (Or yesterday's weather. Or the weather you *wish* were today's weather.)
99. Wings and/or Roots. (Can you integrate both the literal and the figurative?)	100. Create an acrostic.

101. Create an "inchie" for your "current answer" to each of the following words: watching, listening, feeling, eating/drinking, smelling, doing, wearing, thinking, wishing/hoping. Adhere them all to the page and embellish as desired.

102. Your favorite _____ (CD, movie, television show, book, character, food, place, color, animal, flower...)

103. Something you love.

104. Some*one* you love.

105. Something you hate.	106. A particular place.
107. One of your favorite hobbies/ pastimes.	108. _ [Pick a number]_ things you're most grateful for.

Resources:

"Zentangle®" is a specific style of art created by Rick Roberts and Maria Thomas. They describe it as "an easy to learn and relaxing method of creating beautiful images from repetitive patterns." A true tangle consists of "strings" (the "doodly" parts that divide the image into segments) which enclose patterns, and does not depict any actual object/person/etc. If you want to learn true tangling, you can take a class from a Certified Zentangle Teacher® (CZT®), or read one of the books available from authors who are CZT's. Zentangle-inspired art uses a similar style to create an image – which may or may not depict a particular subject. (Visit www.zentangle.com for more information.)

*****

The internet provides a number of recipes for various art supplies – watercolors, alcohol inks, rubber stamp cleaner, Mod Podge™ substitute *(and why you might not want to make it yourself)*, etc. If you're looking for something else in particular, try a search and see if someone has posted DIY instructions!

*****

Use 40% off coupons to get supplies at Michael's and/or JoAnn's. This is an especially good way to get pricier supplies, like gesso.

*****

Craft acrylics and foam brushes can be purchased with 40% off coupons, too, but they also periodically go on sale for pretty cheap. Keep your eyes open and you may be able to save your coupons for higher-ticket items. (I buy spiral-bound watercolor-paper sketchbooks when they go on sale, too, as this is what I use for journaling. And any time I have a 40% off coupon and nothing else I need, I pick up an extra one.)

*****

Stock up on glue sticks when school is starting and they're cheap.

*****

Be sure to protect your table while working on your art journal – especially from permanent marker bleed-through!

*****

And just in case you were wondering…there are no pictures in this book *by design*. I want you to interpret the prompts *your* way, and I don't want my illustrations to short-circuit your creativity, communicating a certain "right way" to complete each one. I welcome you to share your pictures, though! Come by and link up at our Examples page (http://store.titus2homemaker.com/art-journaling-examples/).

About the Author

Rachel Ramey is a stay-at-home wife, and second-generation homeschooling mother of four. She has written a variety of resources for homemakers, homeschoolers, and bloggers/website owners, and blogs regularly at Titus2Homemaker.com. She wrote this book because she, herself, struggles with creative/non-linear thinking, and wanted a means of practicing this skill and teaching it to her daughters.